CORONADO
DREAMER IN
GOLDEN ARMOR

CORONADO
DREAMER IN GOLDEN ARMOR

by William Jay Jacobs

Franklin Watts
New York / Chicago / London / Toronto / Sydney
A First Book

Cover illustration by Amy Wasserman
Cover photograph © New York Public Library, Picture Collection
Cover map copyright © North Wind Picture Archives, Alfred, Me.

Photographs copyright ©: New York Public Library, Picture Collection: pp. 2, 8, 12,
30, 41, 44; Scala/Art Resource, Inc.: p. 14; North Wind Picture Archives: pp. 18, 22,
25, 34, 36, 38, 49, 51, 54; The Library of Congress: p. 20; Photo Researchers, Inc.:
pp. 28 (Daniel Zirinsky), 29 (Kent and Donna Dannen); American Museum of
Natural History: p. 40; Stock Montage/Historical Pictures Service: p. 47;
The Bettmann Archive: p. 56.

Library of Congress Cataloging-in-Publication Data

Jacobs, William Jay.
Coronado: dreamer in golden armor / by William Jay Jacobs
p. cm. — (A First Book)
Includes bibliographical references and index.
ISBN 0-531-20140-6
1. Coronado, Francisco Vásquez de 1510–1554 — Juvenile literature.
2. Explorers — America—Biography—Juvenile literature.
3. Explorers—Spain—Biography—Juvenile literature.
[1. Coronado, Francisco Vásquez de, 1510–1554. 2. Explorers 3. Southwest—New
Discovery and exploration. 4. America—Discovery and exploration.] I. Title.
E125.V3J33 1994
979'.01'092—dc20   93-31174
[B]   CIP AC

CONTENTS

All that glisters is not gold
    — SHAKESPEARE, *The Merchant of Venice*

*Coronado and his men
search for gold and glory.*

PREFACE
TO THE
DREAM

February 22, 1540. From a city in the province of New Spain, now known as Mexico, a man set out at the head of a proud and splendid army in quest of gold. Some of the soldiers on horseback with him even dreamed that beyond the Seven Cities of Gold they sought might lie the wealthy land of India, or perhaps the home of the fabled Kublai Khan, or even the legendary Cathay. Neither they nor the handsome young Spanish leader, who wore a plumed helmet and armor made of glittering gold, had any doubt of their coming success.

And why should they? Just two decades earlier, conquistadore (conqueror) Hernando Cortés had won for Spain the great Aztec empire commanded by Montezuma. Even more recently, another conquistadore, Francisco Pizarro, had gathered whole rooms filled with glittering treasure from his prisoner, Atahualpa, the holy monarch of the Incas in Peru.

Now the Spanish leader Francisco Vásquez de Coronado had every reason to expect success, too. Of noble birth, he was married to a gentle, beautiful woman of great wealth. A daring adventurer, known for his skill as a warrior, Coronado had already won glory in combat. He had served with success as governor of a large, important province of New Spain. Well educated, intelligent and bold, he commanded the most powerful and best-equipped force yet to be gathered in the Americas.

A decade and a half later, Coronado was destined to die an embittered man, considered by many to be a failure. He had returned from his adventure neither with glory nor with gold. Yet we now know that he accomplished much. He recorded his travels through the vast territory of today's southwestern United States. Other explorers and hosts of settlers followed his pathway into New Mexico, Arizona, Texas, Oklahoma, and Kansas. His forces touched upon Lower California. They also discovered the Grand Canyon and the Colorado River.

Coronado left behind him, too, the tale of his contacts with people of the region, such as the Pueblos and the Apaches. The result was a story filled with important new knowledge. It was filled, as well, with high adventure.

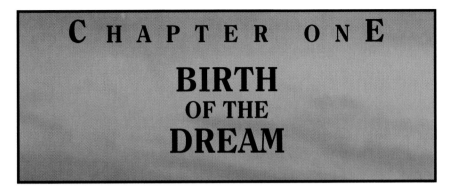

C H A P T E R O N E

BIRTH
OF THE
DREAM

In 1492, while searching for an all-water route to Asia, Christopher Columbus accidentally stumbled upon the Americas. In the years that followed, Spanish explorers in North America, excited by the tales they heard from Indians, searched in vain for the valuable spices of India and the gold of legendary El Dorado. One of those northern adventures, led by Álvar Núñez Cabeza de Vaca, set the stage for Coronado's explorations.

Cabeza de Vaca's journey from Florida into the Gulf of Mexico ended with the near destruction of his entire fleet. He and two other Spaniards were forced into slavery by Indians on the Texas coast, not far from today's Galveston. A fourth member of the surviving group, Estaban, was a black man, a Spanish slave born in Africa.

All four men eventually escaped from their captors, making their way in 1536 to New Galicia, the Spanish province in Mexico where Coronado soon would be gov-

*Although held captive by American Indians,
Cabeza de Vaca escaped to tell his fellow Spaniards
stories of fantastic cities filled with gold and silver.*

12

ernor. There, Cabeza de Vaca told stories he had heard of seven fantastic cities, filled with almost limitless supplies of silver, gold, and precious jewels. These were, he was sure, the Seven Cities of Gold described in ancient stories. Even before that time, the tale of the Seven Cities of Gold was a legend widely shared by Spanish colonists. With the arrival of Cabeza de Vaca in Mexico, the Spaniards were spurred to action.

António de Mendoza, the most powerful figure in the government of New Spain, was determined to send an expedition northward to see whether there really were cities filled with emeralds and gold. To lead the search, Mendoza rejected the offers of Hernando Cortés, the conqueror of Mexico. Instead, he chose his own personal assistant, a young man he treated almost as a son, Francisco Vásquez de Coronado.

Coronado was born into a prominent, wealthy family in Spain, probably in 1510. After receiving a fine formal education, he became an assistant to Mendoza, accompanying the powerful Spanish administrator to Mexico as a private secretary. Two years later, Mendoza helped his young aide marry Doña Beatriz de Estrada, a daughter of one of Mexico's wealthiest and most powerful Spanish families. From that marriage, Coronado gained far more than money or influence. Beatriz proved to be a kind and loving wife, a person who cared deeply for him and whom he would miss desperately once he set out in search of the Seven Cities of Gold.

António de Mendoza

14

With Mendoza's help, Coronado gained both power and experience as a soldier. In 1537, when slaves brought from Africa rose in revolt against the Spaniards, it was Coronado, aided by Indian allies, who put down the rebellion. Afterwards, he hanged several of the black leaders. In October 1538, Coronado was appointed governor of New Galicia, a large province in northwestern Mexico. There, he moved quickly to build roads and to make the towns secure from Indian attacks.

In February 1539, a well-traveled priest, Fray Marcos de Niza (Friar Mark of Nice) set out on a journey from New Galicia, accompanied by Cabeza de Vaca's ambitious black slave Estaban (who had outlived his master). After a few weeks, they returned with a startling tale about an area known as Topira. There, they reported, the Indians "wear emeralds and other precious jewels upon their bodies," along with "strong armor made of silver, fashioned after various shapes of beasts."

Then, in early July, the barefooted Friar Marcos returned alone from another expedition, this time with even more startling news. In a journey through the desert, Estaban had been killed by Indians jealous of his charm and his pride. After that, said Marcos, he alone had continued to explore and had come upon that greatest of all prizes, the Seven Cities of Gold!

To Coronado, the tale told so convincingly by a priest, seemed too wonderful to resist. For the young Spanish adventurer, it stood out as the very chance for glory he always had yearned for so desperately. At once he set out with Fray Marcos for Mexico City. There, he would inform Mendoza of the priest's discovery: wealth perhaps as great as that of India or Cathay, riches that soon might belong to Spain and, in part, to themselves.

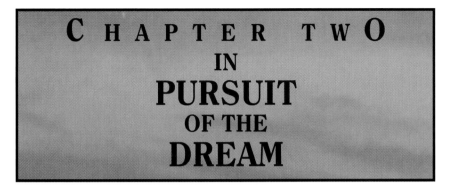

CHAPTER TWO
IN
PURSUIT
OF THE
DREAM

The stories Fray Marcos told about the Seven Cities of Gold threw Mexico City into a frenzy. Hernando Cortés tried desperately to be the one responsible for organizing an expedition to the north. So, too, did another famous explorer Hernando de Soto. But Mendoza had the title of Viceroy and, for the sake of both glory and gold, he was determined to launch his own expedition at once. In command of it would be his trustworthy young favorite, Francisco Vásquez de Coronado.

Barely thirty years old at the time, Coronado had already earned great trust and respect among the Spanish colonists in Mexico. He was considered competent, intelligent, mature, and completely responsible for his actions. Coronado regretted the need to leave his wife behind. Yet he felt a special sense of duty in the expedition. If it succeeded, Spain would become the dominant power in the sixteenth-century world.

To help finance the expedition, Viceroy Mendoza

Mexico City

advanced 60,000 ducats. Coronado, largely with his wife's resources, contributed an additional 50,000 ducats. Other Spaniards also supplied large amounts. Many of the expedition's soldiers came forth with money of their own, hoping to share in the gold and silver they felt certain awaited them to the north. Some of the Spanish troops hoped to win ownership of entire native cities and vast agricultural acreage. In all, the money collected to finance the expedition amounted to several million dollars by today's standards.

On February 22, 1540, Coronado, wearing his brilliant golden armor, stood at the head of a splendid force of 225 cavalrymen and 60 foot soldiers. Behind the soldiers gathered a large voluntary group of Indian warriors, as well as Indian servants and African slaves.

Just before their departure a Catholic mass was said to pray for the safety and success of all those setting out on the mission. Viceroy Mendoza reminded the soldiers of the rewards each of them might receive. He then had the entire force swear obedience to Coronado.

With banners flying, Coronado led his forces forward on what, he and his men were certain, would be a journey of adventure, of glory, and of enormous financial profit.

Almost from the beginning there was trouble: too much baggage, too much equipment, too many burdens that, very soon, were left behind as the warriors made their way northward. Herds of cattle, sheep, and pigs, brought along to feed the soldiers, only slowed the army down.

Before long, in an Indian ambush, Coronado's closest military adviser was pierced by an arrow. Several of the Indian attackers were captured and publicly hanged

Coronado and a group of more than 280
Spanish and Indians set off in search of Cíbola.

from trees. But the loss of Coronado's military leader would prove serious.

Some 300 miles (483 km) north of his starting point, Coronado received startling news. Scouts sent in advance of the main force reported that the stories told by Fray Marcos were untrue! The region to the north, they said, close to Cíbola, was far from rich with gold and silver. The scouts uncovered none of the precious metals. Not only that, the Indians of the region were fiercely hostile to outsiders and, if necessary, willing to fight them to the death.

Fray Marcos, away for a time, soon rejoined Coronado's group and denied the charges. But the doubts of Coronado about the priest's story did not disappear. Instead they continued to grow.

As winter approached, Coronado began to lay out a camp for his soldiers near the town of Culiacán, but Fray Marcos objected. Riches lay ahead, he said. Why should the army wait? The troops should go at once to the Seven Cities of Gold. Finally, Coronado agreed to take some of his men northward to explore the region. Lightly equipped, they could move swiftly and see what actually stood before them.

Almost from the beginning they were disappointed. Indians they came upon knew nothing of the gold that Marcos had described. Meanwhile, there were wide rivers to cross and high hills to climb. Sheep, brought

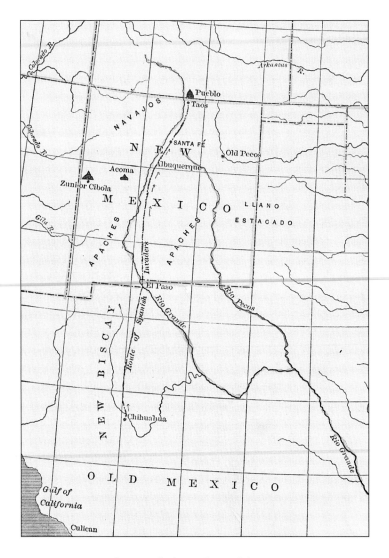

*Coronado traveled northward from Mexico
City into what is now New Mexico.*

along for food, lost their hooves on rock-filled paths and had to be left behind. Soon, the Spanish force found itself trying to live off the countryside from day to day. They encountered rattlesnakes, scorpions, huge lizards, and owls, some of which the adventurers had never seen before. Often there was no grass. Instead, there was cactus everywhere. With little water to be found, many of the horses died, and the men were driven wild with thirst. Proud soldiers were reduced to eating pine nuts and acorns.

Finally, the Spanish force reached what they called Vermilion River, because it was so muddy in color. That river, Coronado knew, was close to Cíbola, the region supposedly containing the Seven Cities of Gold, the goal of his journey. But what should he do? It was in Cíbola that Estaban had been murdered by Indians. Already one band of Indians had tried to ambush Coronado's forces. Yet if he did not go on, his exhausted and hungry men might not survive.

On the morning of July 7, 1540, Coronado ordered his force to move ahead and prepare for deadly combat.

CHAPTER THREE

VICTORY,
FOLLOWED BY
DISAPPOINTMENT

When Coronado reached the supposed Seven Cities of Gold described by Fray Marcos, what must he have thought? Instead of a complex of tall buildings that dwarfed those of Mexico City, there were only scattered structures. Even more important, there was not even a hint of gold!

The Spanish leader had invested much of his wife's and his own fortune in the expedition. He also had staked his reputation as a leader. And now, at the site of a poor Indian village, he faced hostile warriors, who warned him not to advance any farther.

At first, Coronado clad in his golden armor stepped forward, followed by his officers, to speak of peace. Noticing how tired and weak the Spaniards looked from their long journey, the Indians greeted them with arrows. Coronado had no choice. Either he had to press forward, or he and his men would lose their lives.

*A Pueblo Indian looks out
for the invading Spanish forces.*

"*Santiago!*" (St. James!) he cried out, the order for an attack! Drawing their swords, the Spanish soldiers charged into the Indian force, killing many of them. Even Fray Marcos, a man of religion, applauded the assault.

At first, the Indians found safety behind the sturdy walls of their city, but in one place a ladder still stood, and Coronado led the charge toward it. Seeing the Spaniard's golden armor the Indians fired their arrows at him, striking him in the face. Only Coronado's sturdy helmet saved him from heavy stones thrown at him from above.

Along with other wounded Spanish soldiers, Coronado was carried away from the wall. Then, believing that the Indians' supply of stones and arrows must be running low, the invading force attacked once more. This time they succeeded. The Indians fled the scene.

Following their victory, the exhausted and hungry Spaniards searched not for gold and silver but for food. Their triumph had won them only corn and beans.

Coronado soon recovered from his wounds. In a letter to Viceroy Mendoza, he reported how very different the reality of Cíbola was from the claims of Fray Marcos. As he put it, "I can assure your lordship that in reality [Marcos] has not told the truth in a single thing he has said, but everything is the reverse of what he has said, except the name of the city and the large stone houses."

Pedro de Castañeda, one of the Spanish soldiers who kept a careful diary, described Cíbola as "a little, unattractive village."

Before long, Fray Marcos decided to return to Mexico, settling in disgrace in a tiny town. Once highly popular, he was visited for the rest of his life only by a few loyal priests who remained his friends. Eager for fame, eager to be a hero, he had been trapped by going too far in telling his story.

Meanwhile, Coronado, who had found no gold, no silver, no precious jewels, decided to press on with his expedition. Before the year 1540 came to an end, either he or his scouts had explored much of what are today Arizona and New Mexico. They had come upon the Grand Canyon. They had traveled toward the Mississippi River to the east and touched upon California to the west, covering much of what today is the southwestern portion of United States.

Coronado first sent a party westward under Captain Don Pedro de Tovar. Near the San Francisco mountains of Arizona, they came across the fortresslike homes of an Indian tribe known as the Hopi. Captain Tovar succeeded in conquering the Hopi, but he did not stay in the region. Instead, he returned with his men to Coronado's main party, as he had been ordered to do.

Coronado sent another small party under García López de Cárdenas westward into what today is north-

*Coronado was the first European to encounter
the cliff-dwelling Indians of the American Southwest.*

ern Arizona. What they discovered was beyond the
wildest imagination of the Spanish invaders: the Grand
Canyon, a gorge some 300 miles (483 km) long, as
much as 15 miles (25 km) across from side to side, and
1 mile (2 km) deep. No other canyon on Earth is so
spectacular. On hearing of the discovery, Coronado was
enormously impressed. Yet, the discovery was of little
use to the Spaniards. They craved wealth — cities of

Coronado and his party were understandably awed by the majesty of the Grand Canyon.

*Alvarado was sent to explore the lands
that had been described by Bigotes.*

gold and silver. Not knowing that land to the far west, particularly southern California, was rich in the very metals he sought, Coronado turned eastward.

One day he was visited by a tall, handsome chieftain from the Indian village of Cicuyé. Because of the thin moustache he wore, the Spaniards soon came to call him "Bigotes" (meaning "whiskers"). After Coronado and Bigotes exchanged gifts, the Indian drew pictures of hump-backed animals, known today as buffalo. He also told stories that reminded Coronado of Cabeza de Vaca's tales of gold.

Coronado quickly sent another bold warrior, Hernando de Alvarado, eastward to explore the lands Bigotes had described. Alvarado found no gold. But on September 7, 1540, he suddenly came upon a wide river, known today as the Rio Grande. Alvarado also recognized the nearby lands he had discovered as rich and fertile, ideal for farming. In a message to Coronado, he suggested that the Spanish forces perhaps should spend the winter along the river.

While waiting for a reply, Alvarado rested. He also asked Bigotes to accompany him eastward to see the buffalo creatures. The Indian chief replied that he could not be gone from his people for so long. As a substitute, he offered a captive, a man who knew the area to the east very well.

The clever young Indian he presented to Alvarado

wore a headdress that resembled the turbans worn by
people in Turkey. Because of that, the Spaniards named
him El Turco (The Turk). El Turco became the second
great storyteller to cross the path of Coronado. Just as
the tales of Fray Marcos had inspired the Spanish
adventurers to explore to the north and east, now the
false words of El Turco would set the future direction of
Coronado's dreams.

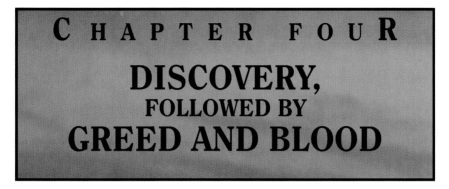

CHAPTER FOUR

DISCOVERY,
FOLLOWED BY
GREED AND BLOOD

While Coronado, under the influence of El Turco, sought riches to the north and east, Viceroy Mendoza, at home in Mexico City, tried loyally to help him in the west.

One group of Mendoza's explorers, headed by Hernando de Alarcón, sailed up what is known today as the Gulf of California. Alarcón eventually discovered the mouth of the Colorado River. Continuing upriver, he tried to make contact with Coronado, not knowing how very far east the Spanish force had gone.

Frustrated and embarrassed by his failure to find Coronado, Alarcón returned to Mexico City. His journey, however, had not been a failure. He had succeeded in discovering for the first time that Lower California, contrary to what always had been believed, was not an island, but rather a peninsula.

Meanwhile, Coronado had sent another explorer, Captain Melchor Díaz, southward to meet Alarcón. Díaz arrived too late, but like Alarcón, he discovered that

33

While Coronado traveled northward, Hernando de Alarcón moved along the Gulf of California to the northwest, where he discovered that Lower California was a peninsula and not an island.

Lower California was a peninsula, not an island. And he, too, reached the banks of the Colorado River, becoming the first European to find a land route from Mexico to California. Regrettably, before returning to Coronado's camp, he died from injuries he received in an accident on horseback.

The discoveries of Díaz and Alarcón took place late in 1540. Yet it was not until 1701, following the journey of a Jesuit priest, that European mapmakers finally came to accept that Lower California was, indeed, not an island.

Although Spanish explorers had succeeded in their journeys to the west, Coronado saw things differently. Under the influence of El Turco, he believed that gold, if it was to be found at all, would be found by traveling eastward.

One after another, the Spanish leaders questioned the young captive, El Turco. The more they questioned him, the more they came to believe his stories. Great wealth, especially gold, he assured them, lay in the wonderful land of Quivira. In that land, declared El Turco, people rode in canoes with oarlocks and figureheads made of gold. The king of Quivira, he said, napped under a tree from whose branches dangled golden ornaments. Even the servants had on their tables silver serving pieces and golden dishes, pitchers, and bowls.

As final "proof," El Turco confided to Coronado that, after capturing him, Bigotes had taken from him a

Imprisoning Indians and stealing their food, the
Spaniards camped for the winter at Kuaua Pueblo,
which is today a part of Coronado State Park, New Mexico.

pair of golden bracelets. When the Spaniards demanded
to see the bracelets, the leaders of Cicuyé only laughed.
El Turco, they charged, was a liar. There had been no
gold bracelets, and Quivira, too, was a land without
gold. So great was the golden dream of Coronado and
his companions that, no matter how unlikely the tales
of El Turco seemed to be, they continued to believe him.

As a result, the Spaniards clamped Bigotes and the other chief of Cicuyé in chains.

By that act, they had achieved for El Turco the first of his goals, vengeance on the tribesmen who had enslaved him. El Turco was certain that, in time, the Spaniards, too, would be punished.

After imprisoning the two leaders, the Spanish forces inflicted still more cruelty on the Indians, ancestors of today's Pueblo people. Seeking shelter from the winter cold, the conquistadores drove the natives from their homes, even taking their food. Coronado had his soldiers seize warm blankets and clothing from the Indians.

The tribesmen fought back, seizing forty of the Spaniards' horses. In revenge, Spanish soldiers under Cárdenas attacked an Indian fortress, taking more than one hundred Indians prisoner. Although the victors had promised their captives peace, Cárdenas ordered them tied to stakes and set afire. Seeing their comrades burning to death, other Indians charged, trying to destroy the burning stakes, but the Spaniards brutally cut many of the rescuers to death with swords.

When Coronado himself learned what had happened he was displeased, embarrassed. He expressed his sorrow to the natives. But he did not punish Cárdenas.

Coronado then laid siege to the town. Some two hundred Indians were killed. Others fled to the frozen banks of the nearby Rio Grande. Some escaped, but

Many Indians tried to escape from the invading Spanish by running to the banks of the frozen Rio Grande. However, they were eventually captured and murdered.

many met death at the hands of Spanish swordsmen. At a nearby village, the Spaniards killed almost all the men and turned the women and children into slaves. They then looted the village and burned it to the ground. In his search for gold, the noble young leader, Francisco Vásquez de Coronado, had become drenched in human blood.

CHAPTER FIVE

GOLD
AND
LIES

Spring 1541. As the ice and snow of winter faded and spring arrived, Coronado began to prepare to travel eastward. There, he felt certain, would be the true reward: the golden city of Quivira. Meanwhile, El Turco cleverly built upon his earlier stories, telling the Spaniards even more about the spectacular wealth that lay before them.

On April 23, 1541, Coronado departed for the east, setting out with his entire force of 1,500 men, along with many sheep and cattle. As the Spaniards set out, Coronado removed the shackles from his prisoners, Bigotes and the Cicuyé chieftain, and set them free.

As El Turco later told his story, it was at that time he secretly met with the two Cicuyé leaders, along with other warriors, and told them of his plan. He would lead the Spaniards out into the trackless plains where there was little food or water, and in that wilderness all the white men would die. But, for then at least, his plan remained a secret.

39

*Coronado and his band marched on searching
in vain for the golden city of Quivira.*

Soon after setting out, the Spaniards encountered for the first time the enormous herds of buffalo that roamed the land. Castañeda, the faithful journal keeper, described the animals in his diary:

From the middle of the body toward the rear they are covered with very fine woolly hair like the mane of a wild lion. They have a hump larger than that of a camel and their horns, which barely show through the hair, are short and thick.

At first, the Spaniards' horses greatly feared the strange animals. One Spanish soldier remembered reading of Marco Polo's meeting with yaks, humpbacked cattle with long wool. Were they, he wondered, really in Asia, perhaps in Tibet or the Gobi desert? Whatever the truth, the conquistadores knew that scarcely a day would pass without their sighting great herds of buffalo.

Not long after their departure, the Spaniards came across a new band of Indians, tribesmen they spoke of as

The first drawing of a bison made around 1553.

Teyas, or "Texas" Indians. The Spaniards did not know that the word teyas meant simply "friends," a polite form of greeting. From that mistake, came the name today of the state of Texas.

By the end of May, the Spanish force was in trouble. They were short of food, and there was almost no water to drink. The Teyas Indians also warned the Spaniards that El Turco had lied to them, that Quivira lay much farther to the north, and that the people living there were not rich, but poor.

Coronado decided to find out for himself. He chose his finest warriors, thirty horsemen and six foot soldiers, and set out to explore the pathway described by the Teyas tribesmen. Many of the other soldiers objected, worried that Coronado would deny them the gold that surely lay ahead. But Coronado assured them they would receive their share.

For more than a month, the small Spanish party pushed ahead across what today are the states of Texas and Oklahoma, finally crossing into the heart of Kansas. At the end of June, they stumbled upon a small, frightened band of Quivira Indians. Unlike the wealthy tribesmen El Turco had described, they indeed were poor, wearing simple clothing and living on buffalo meat.

Then, at last, El Turco confessed. What he had wanted, first of all, was freedom from his Cicuyé captors. After that he had planned to lead the Spaniards into distant, isolated prairies where, without food or water, they all would die. He had expected to escape much earlier, but he had been watched too carefully. Meanwhile, the white men had been surviving by shooting buffalo. He now admitted not knowing at all where there might be gold.

Coronado could have executed El Turco at once. Instead, he clamped the Indian into irons and moved him along with his small band of Spanish soldiers.

Soon afterward the Spaniards reached Quivira. They found no golden-clad chieftain, no golden houses, no golden decorated canoes, no precious jewels. Instead, there were only small cabins covered with grass, clay, and straw. The aging, trembling tribal chief wore around his neck a simple ornament of copper.

Still, Coronado acted formally. He claimed all the land of the region in the name of the king of Spain and had all the people there pledge their loyalty to the Spanish monarch. This, at least in name, added another province to the royal domain of his native land. In a journey of some 3,000 miles (4,828 km) from Mexico City, Coronado had reached a point approximately the center of what today is the United States.

But what would Coronado do now? Where would be go next? It was time, he finally decided, to return to Mexico. But first, he had El Turco questioned in detail. Coronado discovered that, even as a captive, El Turco had tried to persuade his native countrymen to attack the Spanish explorers and to kill them all. The night

Hernando de Soto

before leaving the "City of God," Coronado finally
ordered El Turco's execution. Spanish soldiers bound
the Indian and placed a rope around his neck. Then they
choked him to death.

Disappointed and discouraged by what had happened to them, Coronado and his Spanish warriors slowly made their way back to the west. They made no attempt to find and execute Bigotes, who also had betrayed them. Nor did they know that traveling from Florida and only some 300 miles (483 km) away from them, Hernando de Soto had come upon the powerful Mississippi River. The two expeditions, nearly spanning the entire North American continent, were destined never to meet.

Meanwhile, winter had come again. And this time, because nearly all the Indians had come to see the Spanish as their enemies, there lay ahead for the conquistadores only a season of bitter cold and hunger.

The search for gold had failed.

C H A P T E R   S I X

RETURN
TO
MEXICO

Coronado did what he could to relieve the disappointment and growing depression of his soldiers. He promised that, in the spring, when it was warm once again, the army would return to Quivira and search for gold. But, it was not to be.

On December 27, 1541, a holiday time for the Spaniards, Coronado rode on horseback beside a companion, Captain Don Rodrigo Maldonado. For pleasure, the two men began to race. The leather band that held Coronado's saddle, probably rotted from age, suddenly burst. The Spanish commander was thrown to the ground just where Maldonado's horse was passing. Francisco Vásquez de Coronado was struck on the head by the horse's hoof. For days he lingered near death.

He survived, but never again would be the same. Even afterward he would be sick and uncertain, weak in both body and mind. Very possibly his brain had been damaged.

When Coronado was a young man in Spain, an

In defeat and with his reputation for courage in decline,
Coronado led his men on the long march back to Mexico City.
For much of the journey, he was carried on a stretcher.

astrologer friend had once read his fortune. The prediction was that he would become rich, famous, and powerful, but that one day he would fall from his horse and never recover. Coronado always had remembered the prophecy and concluded that the seer had indeed been correct.

Expecting to die, Coronado decided to lead his soldiers quickly back to Mexico, where at least he could be with his wife and children. Some of his officers wanted to continue the search for gold, but Coronado refused.

As a result, the Spanish leader's reputation for courage declined. Many of his men stopped obeying his commands. Three of the religious missionaries in the group finally notified him that they would not return to Mexico. Instead, they would stay on, giving their lives if necessary to win the souls of Indians to the teachings of Jesus. The fate of two of the missionaries remains uncertain. But, the third, Fray Juan de Padilla, soon became a martyr. While his two companions watched helplessly, Indians filled Fray Juan's head with arrows, threw his body into a pit, and heaped rocks upon the corpse.

In April 1541, Coronado and his men began their journey home. During much of the retreat to Mexico, Coronado was unable to ride on horseback and had to be carried on a stretcher drawn by a pair of mules. Often, as the Spanish troops made their way southward,

Fray Juan de Padilla, a martyr to the cause of spreading Christianity among the Indians of the American Southwest

Indians let loose frightening yells at them, tried to stab their horses at night, and fired poisoned arrows at the conquistadores who so often had been brutal to them.

The clothing of the once proud army was reduced to rags. Most of the men were filthy with lice. Many horses collapsed and died. Some of the Spaniards never reached Mexico City. Dreading the charges of failure that would greet them on their return, they left the caravan, most choosing to live the remainder of their lives at places along the way, mostly in northern Mexico.

At last, fewer than one hundred tired, discouraged soldiers reached the capital city. Coronado, still in poor health from his fall, came face to face with Viceroy Mendoza, who had provided much of his personal fortune to finance the failed expedition. All of that money, of course, was lost. Many other Spaniards, too, had put vast amounts of money into the venture.

In time, Mendoza forgave Coronado for what had happened, allowing his former favorite to stay on for two more years as governor of New Galicia. And even after that, Coronado continued to serve as a royal official.

In August 1544, Coronado's performance as an officer was examined, something that was done for all Spanish officials. Some of those who had served with Coronado on the expedition accused him of bad management, of cruelty to the Indians, and of taking Indian property. As a result, some of Coronado's personal pos-

For nearly ten years after his return,
Coronado and his family lived in a magnificent
palace near the center of Mexico City.

sessions were seized. For a short time, he was forced to stay at home and not to meet with other people. Soon afterward, however, he became a member of the town council in Mexico City. In 1546, a royal panel headed by Viceroy Mendoza completely rejected all charges made against him for his supposed mishandling of the expedition.

For ten more years, Coronado and his family lived in a magnificent mansion near the center of Mexico City, from time to time visiting their beautiful country estates. Coronado and Mendoza remained close friends, and the leader of the failed expedition to the north gave his wholehearted support to the viceroy's policies. The Spanish government gave thanks to Coronado for his expedition by presenting him with several Indian servants. The town council of Mexico City also honored him for his many years of service.

In the autumn of 1544, Francisco Vásquez de Coronado died. At the time, he was forty-four years old.

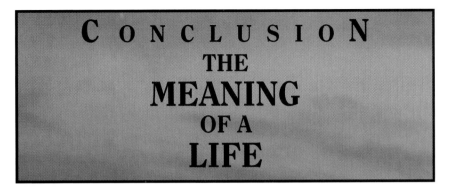

CONCLUSION
THE
MEANING
OF A
LIFE

What did Coronado accomplish? What was the meaning of his life?

Perhaps it is most important to remember that Coronado was a man with a dream, a goal. True, his goal had about it a degree of selfishness: to find riches in gold and to claim the prize for New Spain and for himself, just as previous Spanish adventurers in the Americas had seized the incredible treasures of the Aztecs and the Incas.

Coronado did not achieved that goal, yet he and his forces had accomplished much. Although they returned without treasure, their expedition had succeeded in answering many of the mysteries concerning lands to the north of Mexico. They had traveled along the Colorado, Kansas, and Arkansas Rivers. They had discovered the mile-deep Grand Canyon. They had met and formed relationships with great Indian peoples, such as the Pueblos and the Apaches. Spanish missionaries

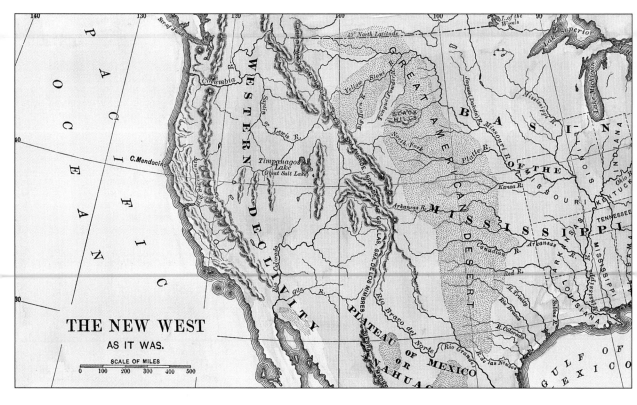

The journey of Francisco Vásquez de Coronado

remained to spread the story of Jesus Christ and Christianity.

Later explorers made their way along the trails of Kansas, Arizona, Texas, Oklahoma, New Mexico, and southern California. It was Coronado and the Spanish soldiers connected with his expedition, however, who first touched upon those lands in what today is the

United States of America. Those who came afterward were the pioneers. Coronado and his men were the *discoverers*.

It is true that no gold was found as a result of Coronado's journey. Many of the Indian tribes he first encountered greeted later explorers with poisoned arrows. Mexicans who supplied money to Coronado and his men were angry to have lost their investments.

Still, after Coronado's expedition returned to Mexico, the lands he had visited no longer remained a mystery. Their people and their resources at least were known. What is today the American Southwest finally had been revealed to outsiders.

A brave commander who inspired the loyalty of his forces, Coronado proved to be competent in the handling of details. Following his accident on horseback, he lost much of his physical and mental strength. He left the new territories he had discovered before his task there was completed. Yet, even after returning to Mexico in failure, he continued to play a role in public affairs, to be part of Spanish life in his society.

Other men followed in the path of Francisco Vásquez de Coronado. Juan Rodriguez Cabrillo explored the coast of California by sea, reaching it two years after Coronado's assistant, Alarcón. Juan de Oñate and his forces conquered the Pueblo Indians. Later, Father Junípero Serra introduced the Catholic religion to Indians of New Mexico, Arizona, and

Junípero Serra

California, while also showing them how to cultivate oranges, grapes, and olives. Father Serra, too, brought white settlers and the Indians together to live side by side in Spanish missions.

Yet Coronado had been first. Seeking gold, he was destined to open the way to approximately one fourth of the territory that today makes up the United States. And that, perhaps, was his most lasting accomplishment, the true meaning of his life.

IMPORTANT DATES

1492	Columbus accidentally stumbles upon the Americas.
1510	Probable date of Coronado's birth.
1537	Coronado puts down rebellion of African slave leaders against Spanish authorities in Mexico.
1538	Coronado appointed governor of New Galicia province in northwestern Mexico.
1539	Fray Marcos de Niza and Estaban set out to find Seven Cities of Gold.
1540–February	Coronado launches his splendid army on mission in search of precious metals reported by Marcos.
1540–July	Coronado's forces triumphant at Cíbola, supposed center of Seven Cities of Gold; find Marcos' stories of great wealth vastly exaggerated.
1540–Summer	Parties of explorers from Coronado's armies visit the Grand Canyon, California, and Arizona.
1540–September	Spanish troops commanded by Alvarado come upon the Rio Grande; clever young Indian called "El Turco" (the Turk) by the Spaniards, urges them to seek riches to the north and east.
1540–Winter	Spaniards come into conflict with Cicuyé Indians, killing many of the men and turning women and children into slaves.
1541–Spring	Still hopeful, Coronado leads his army eastward into today's Texas, Oklahoma, and Kansas; Coronado is deeply disappointed to find no riches at Quivira, the supposed "golden city."
1541–December	Coronado injured in horseback race.
1542–April	Spaniards begin their journey home to Mexico City.

Continued on the following page

1544	Coronado's performance as commanding officer examined by Spanish authorities; some of his personal possessions taken from him.
1546	Royal panel reviews and then rejects all charges against Coronado.
1544–Autumn	Coronado dies.

FOR FURTHER READING

FOR OLDER READERS

Bolton, Herbert E. *Coronado, Knight of Pueblos and Plains*. Alburquerque, N.M.: University of New Mexico Press, 1990.

Day, Arthur G. *Coronado's Quest: The Discovery of the Southwestern States*. Westport, Conn.: Greenwood Publishing Group, Inc., 1982.

Hammond, George P. and Rey, Agapito. *Narratives of the Coronado Expedition*. New York: AMS Press, 1977.

FOR MIDDLE READERS

Stein, R. Conrad. *Francisco de Coronado: Explorer of the American Southwest*. Chicago: Childrens Press, 1992.

Zadra, Dan. *Explorers of America: Coronado*. Mankato, M.N.: Creative Education, Inc., 1988.

INDEX

ABOUT
THE
AUTHOR

William Jay Jacobs has studied history at Harvard, Yale, and Princeton and holds a doctorate from Columbia. He has held fellowships with the Ford Foundation and the National Endowment for the Humanities and served as a Fulbright Fellow in India. In addition to broad teaching experience in public and private secondary schools, he has taught at Rutgers University, at Hunter College, and at Harvard. Dr. Jacobs presently is Visiting Fellow in the Department of History at Yale.

Among his previous books for young readers are biographies of such diverse personalities as Abraham Lincoln, Eleanor Roosevelt, Edgar Allan Poe, Hannibal, Hitler, and Mother Teresa. His *America's Story* and *History of the United States* are among the nation's most widely used textbooks.

In the Franklin Watts First Book series, he is the author of *Magellan, Cortés, Pizarro, La Salle, Champlain,* and *Coronado.*